PHINEAS PARKHURST QUIMBY

Revealer of Spiritual Healing to this Age

HIS LIFE
AND
WHAT HE TAUGHT

(Based on the Quimby Manuscripts and original letters in the Library of Congress)

By
ANN BALLEW HAWKINS

DeVORSS & CO., *Publishers*
P.O. Box 550
Marina Del Rey, CA 90291

Copyright, 1951
By Ann Ballew Hawkins

First Printing, 1951
Second Printing, 1952
Third Printing, 1960
Fourth Printing, 1970
Fifth Printing, 1974
Sixth Printing, 1976
All Rights Reserved

ISBN: 0-87516-024-7

Printed in the United States of America by
DeVORSS & Co., P.O. Box 550, Marina Del Rey, CA 90291

FOREWORD

BECAUSE OF THE LACK OF INFORMATION generally on the life of Phineas Parkhurst Quimby, these authentic facts are presented with a sincere desire to bring a very great man into the light of common day. It is an attempt to show Phineas Parkhurst Quimby as his patients and students saw him.

Many of the details of his life have vanished forever, but in dealing with his life, I have taken the safe course of basing it on contemporary *documents*.

Most of this research was done in the New York City Public Library, and the Library of Congress, both places being a gold mine of information for those who seek their hidden treasures.

In preparing the text for this booklet, I have made free use of Horatio Dresser's book, "The Quimby Manuscripts—Showing the Discovery of Spiritual Healing." Horatio Dresser was a son of Julius A. Dresser, who was a student of Dr. Quimby.

I have also used material from Annetta Gertrude Dresser's book, "The Philosophy of P. P. Quimby," published in Boston, 1895. In many instances passages from these books have been copied verbatim.

The original Quimby Manuscripts are in the Library of Congress at Washington, D. C. A great number of copybooks dictated by Dr. Quimby, and written by members of his family are also in the Library of Congress, and are available for research under "Library Restrictions."

I have made an extensive study of the original manuscripts of Dr. Quimby. These were published by Horatio Dresser in 1921, but are now out of print. Also, credit is given to an article appearing in the New England magazine 1888, showing how Dr. Quimby discovered spiritual healing.

For many years the Quimby manuscripts were kept under lock and key by his heirs. Dr. Horatio Dresser persuaded them to place the manuscripts in the Library of Congress, along with letters of gratitude written to Dr. Quimby by a former student. In a circular to the sick which Dr. Quimby wrote while in Portland, Me., he said, "As my practice is unlike all medical practice, it is necessary to say I give no medicine, make no outward applications." Dr. Horatio Dresser stated that Dr. Quimby early began the practice of treating silently and *at a distance*.

Dr. Raymond Chas. Barker, in a recent class, spoke of Dr. Quimby's keen perception, his psychic ability, saying that when a person came into the presence of the great healer, he would announce what the person came for, and what was ailing the patient. (Matt. 12:25)

Dr. Quimby was sure that he had solved the riddle of life and ultimately the whole world would accept his ideas.

His consuming desire was to put it into writing, to teach it, and transmit it to posterity.

He had one fear and only one, and that was, lest he should pass on before the Truth had made a last impress. Dr. Quimby used to say that people sent for him and the undertaker at the same time and the one who got there first got the case.

Although this Truth that he taught is that we are *spiritual* beings actually living in the ETERNAL NOW, time with its limitations, seems a more convenient arrangement, and since "time" has seemed to supersede the idea of eternity in the thought of man, so bent on a material existence, he has also believed himself a creator on his own, with a physical life, entirely independent from God, in whom St. Paul said, "we live, and move, and have our being." (Acts 17:28) As this material design or idea was the *status quo* of the majority of mankind, Dr. Quimby used a repetitious style, a hammering process to drive home his convictions to humanity. Instead of man's being a worm of the dust, a material composition, Dr. Quimby, like Jesus, taught that man is a direct expression of God, his every action, his very being, the "I am" or Ego of man depending wholly on the ONE and ONLY GREAT "I AM," never separated, but a part of the eternal and divine LIFE. (Heb. 3:14)

I have added *all* Bible citations (sometimes repetitiously) in *most* instances to bring out the parallel significance of the scriptures, and to show more clearly that Dr. Quimby used only the word of God as his guide, which was the only source of inspiration in all his teachings and writings.

Ann Ballew Hawkins

Phineas Parkhurst Quimby
HIS LIFE AND WHAT HE TAUGHT

AMONG ALL THE EARLY AMERICAN HEALERS and philosophers, Phineas Parkhurst Quimby's reputation stands the highest for beauty of character and honesty of purpose.

He was born in Lebanon, New Hampshire, February 16th, 1802.

He was a clock maker by trade, and worked at this successfully for many years.

Dr. Quimby sincerely believed that he had come across the method of healing so effectively employed by Jesus and His disciples.

The particular significance of his theory is the basis it affords for the explanation of disease in the light of its inmost origin and cure.

During the years between 1840 and 1866, he referred to his theory as "Science of Health, The Principle, Truth, Science of Christ," and once or twice as "Christian Science." Scores of times, he referred to it as the "Science of Christ."

While the term "Christian Science" was entirely original with Dr. Quimby, it was used by Dr. Deletsche, a German scholar, and was also used in a poem by Abram Cowles, published in 1840. Dr. Quimby was a great student of the Bible, but no reader of philosophy, so could not have borrowed any ideas from Swedenborg, Berkeley or Hegel.

PHINEAS PARKHURST QUIMBY

Dr. Quimby used the term "Christian Science" to signify the exact principles implied in the teachings of Jesus, and also exemplified in his own works among the sick. He once stated that the word, "Science" was used once in the Old Testament and once in the New Testament. (Dan. 1:4) (I Tim. 6:20)

In the early initial stage of Dr. Quimby's research, between 1838 and 1840, he experimented with mesmerism, and it was here that he discovered that pain was in the mind, a false mental concept. While his beginning was crude, his eager desire for truth led him to a point where such elementary pioneer work was no longer necessary, for he discovered *spiritual* Truth through experiment, patient research, and revelation. In 1840 he found a Principle which was not of man himself. Its character was goodness and intelligence. It was the INDWELLING Christ.

He used to say, "When I believed in mesmerism my knowledge was of this world, and not of Truth." He found disease to be an erroneous state of mind, and on this discovery founded a system of treating the sick and founded a Science of Life.

Dr. Quimby's great conviction was that there is a *spiritual* Science superior to the most exact of the natural sciences, which is the basis of all true knowledge, and the source of all true wisdom.

He often said, "Who is the founder of this Science?" And *always* answered, "Jesus Christ."

HIS LIFE AND WHAT HE TAUGHT

Dr. Quimby proved the truth of his teaching by his daily work. The marvelous cures he effected were undeniable evidence of his superior knowledge and skill in applying it for the benefit of suffering humanity. His only interest in his patients was to make them well.

He claimed to be a common everyday man not with superior power over ordinary man. He did not use medicine or any other material agency, nor call to his aid mesmerism in any way whatever, but worked upon scientific principles, the philosophy of which was perfectly explained by him and understood by the patient.

His treatments consisted in an explanation to the patient and the explanation for his system of healing based on eternal principles was capable of being understood.

Accepting his theory, based wholly on the teachings of Jesus, man rises superior to circumstances.

Man is completely at the mercy of his body and its slave if he allows that it is subject to disease. Instead of treating the body as an intelligent organization with independent life, he found Life and Intelligence in consciousness, or the inner man, who occupies the body. He taught that body was but the shadow of the inner scientific man—an imitation of the real everlasting substance, not seen by the physical eye. He never admitted disease only as a deception, a belief of the devil who was a liar from the beginning. (John

8:44) He firmly believed the body to be the garment of thought, portraying the condition of the mind. This outer garment, the natural man as Dr. Quimby called him, is *redeemed* by the Truth that man is made in the image and likeness of God.

His system was based on eternal principles and as capable of being explained as the science of astronomy, mathematics, or music.

Instead of telling a patient he was not sick, Dr. Quimby sat beside him, and explained to him what sickness was, how he got into the condition by accepting false beliefs, or the inventions of the natural or carnal man, and how he could be taken out of it through understanding and recognition of the indwelling Christ, which is the real spiritual man and the only Life of each of us. (John 8:32)

So convinced was he that the same Wisdom and Power which he used to heal the sick was latent in all individuals, that he believed each man could become his own physician and apply the Science of Life in the cure of disease.

He thoroughly believed that all disease should be overcome, since it was the product of ignorance and superstition, and never had any foundation except in belief. (Eccl. 7:29)

Dr. Quimby was often asked what he called his cures. He answered, "The effect of Science because I know how I do them. If I did not know, they would be a mystery to the world and myself."

HIS LIFE AND WHAT HE TAUGHT

Dr. Quimby taught that man's life—and senses, i.e., taste, touch, smell, hearing, and seeing, are in Mind or God and not in matter. (Gen. 1:27) (Rom. 10:17) (John 1:4) (Rom. 8:8, 9)

For more than twenty years he devoted himself to the healing of the sick. (John 14:12)

His most active and constructive period was in Portland, Maine, between 1859 and 1866.

His object was so pure and method so unselfish that when understood, he claimed the favorable attention of all.

Dr. Quimby treated at least 12,000 patients, mostly poor and ailing. He sat with more than three hundred individuals every year for many years. The last five years of his practice he averaged five hundred yearly. He healed people with all sorts of diseases, and in every possible state of mind, brought on by all kinds of false beliefs or inventions of man, dominated by error, and believed to be true. (John 9:33) (Jas. 5:15) He rebuked and cast out sickness with authority and helped thousands with the same Christ Power which Jesus said was within all of us.

He lifted disease from its pretended basis of truth and placed it on its proper basis of error. Some illnesses were occasioned by the belief that the sufferer had committed the unpardonable sin. When he asked what it was, no two persons ever answered alike.

His teachings were not to establish a religious creed, but the outpouring of a Truth that sees the sick cast into prison for no other cause than a belief in the opinions of man.

While not a member of a church or sect, Dr. Quimby had a deeply religious nature, holding firmly to God as the first Cause and fully believing in immortality and probation and progression after death.

He considered his philosophy one which understood would make men free, and independent of all creeds, and laws of man.

He kept no accounts and made no charges for many years, and would never accept pay unless the patient was healed. He was always delighted and flattered at any opportunity to spread his gospel.

He was fortunate enough to be endowed with an original intuitive mind, and a love of truth which stood him in good stead, and enabled him to lay hold of principles which had hitherto eluded the ken of the educated world of that day. The disciples of Jesus were not scholarly men. Jesus was a carpenter. Spirituality does not depend on academic or worldly education. Dr. Quimby wrote no books, but many hundreds of original and logical articles, all in manuscript form.

Before Dr. Quimby ever undertook any writings, he formulated those healing principles sufficiently to communicate a knowledge of them to his disciples.

In his writings there was a sense of repose based on firm conviction, which shows how strong was his

HIS LIFE AND WHAT HE TAUGHT

ideal of health and happiness, and how clear his understanding of life's actual conditions, and man's genuine status as a spiritual being in contrast to the false opinion held by so many that man is the unlikeness of God. Simplicity and sincerity marked all his efforts. With him there was no straining after ideals, no overdrawn affirmations and assertions. He was eminently practical and devoted to the needs of the eternal now.

No single article that Dr. Quimby wrote did his theory full justice, for to those who knew him and received direct benefit from his work, his own life was far larger and nobler than anything he wrote.

If he was unable to complete his "Science of Health" he at least gave great impetus to others and this personal inspiration is perhaps the greatest blessing a man can bestow upon his fellows.

He was never considered a mesmerist, or a charlatan, but a genuine friend to the sick, and by hundreds of his patients he was looked upon as a worker of miracles. Edwin Reed, an ex-mayor of Bath, Maine, declared that Dr. Quimby cured him of total blindness.

When he left Portland, Maine, to make his home in Belfast, Maine, there appeared in the leading newspaper a tribute of appreciation and respect. According to this article, he had manifested wonderful power in healing the sick among the people that no well-informed and unprejudiced person could deny, and he possessed extraordinary ability in detecting the hidden causes of suffering.

He gave freely of all he had and if anyone evinced any particular interest in his theory, he would lend his manuscripts and allow his writings to be copied. His humility seemed to have been equalled only by his native purity of heart.

Dr. Warren F. Evans, student of Dr. Quimby, said that Dr. Quimby's character was noble, his aims pure, a modest and great soul. Had he been of a sordid and grasping nature, he might have acquired wealth, but for that he seemed to have no desire. He made no effort to advertise his theories or to capitalize on them in any way.

He was willing to be misunderstood, charged with putting down religion, or criticized in any other way, if only he could make it clear that there was a pathway to the Science he had found.

Dr. Evans wrote several books on the subject. There was a difference in terminology, but Dr. Quimby's original ideas, couched in Dr. Evans own words.

The following is taken from Dr. Evan's book, "Soul and Body":—"The thought of the Spirit is Life and peace; thinking on the level with the body is death. (Rom. 8:6, 7)

When we find our *real* self, every thing afterwards is easy. No weapon will hurt the *real* self of man, no

HIS LIFE AND WHAT HE TAUGHT

fire will burn it, no wind will dry it up. If we know this we shall grieve not over *appearances.*

All ideas have an inherent tendency to actualize or externalize themselves in the so called material organism. All substance (the unseen) takes form. Thought and existence are identical so it follows to think rightly is to be well and happy.

Mind is the substance. Hence the outer form is to me what I think it to be. (Prov. 23:7) It should be the aim to elevate the Principle of thought above the senses, and be free from their disturbing influences.

Activity of Mind is the only Power and Causal agent in the universe. Ideas are the only real things —Christ is the Alpha and Omega, the first and the last and all between the extremes. (Col. 3:11)

Recognize and *believe* that *in the Christ* or Spirit we are already saved. (Isa. 45:22) (John 3:17) (I Tim. 2:4)

We need to close the senses to the external world of shadow and turn our thoughts inward toward the light of the unseen and *real* world."

Horatio Dresser was given permission to print the Quimby manuscripts in full in 1921. This book is the most important contribution to the subject of spiritual healing ever published. Mr. Dresser and his wife were both healed by Dr. Quimby and were ardent and loyal students.

Mary Baker Eddy, who was then Mrs. Patterson, was also a patient and student of Dr. Quimby from

1862 to 1864, and as such gave him full credit for curing her and teaching her his theories. "On his rare humanity and sympathy" said Mrs. Patterson, "one could write a sonnet." At the time of his death she wrote a poem to Dr. Quimby, who she said, "healed with the Truth that Christ taught." The poem in part, "Potent o'er all, the captive to unbind. To heal the sick, the faint, the halt, and the blind."

In all her letters to Dr. Quimby, covering a period from 1862 to 1864, she gave him full credit for discovering and reducing spiritual healing to a *Science*. Her letters were overfull of fulsome acknowledgement of her indebtedness to him for the help he gave her mind as well as healing her body.

On Jan. 12, 1863, she wrote Dr. Quimby that she was to all who saw her a living monument of his power, and that she ate, drank and was merry, with no laws to fetter her spirit. She added that she was as much an escaped prisoner as her dear husband (Major Glover) was. She also stated that her explanation of Dr. Quimby's curative Principle surprised people, especially those whose minds were all matter. The letter was written from Sanbornton Bridge, New Hampshire.[1]

Mrs. Patterson wrote the Portland, Me., Courier a letter on November 7, 1862, that she could perceive, dimly at first, and only as trees walking, the great Principle which supported Dr. Quimby's works;

1. Original letter in Library of Congress.

HIS LIFE AND WHAT HE TAUGHT

and just in the degree of her understanding of Truth was her recovery and his explanation, when understood cured the patient.

The Portland, Me., Advertiser published another message of Nov. 8, 1862, that P. P. Quimby stood upon the plain of wisdom with his Truth. She added that Christ healed the sick but not with drugs, and that Dr. Quimby spoke as no man had spoken and healed as no man had ever healed since the time of Christ. She also stated that P. P. Quimby rolled away the stone from the sepulchre of error, and health was the resurrection.

In another letter to Dr. Quimby Mrs. Patterson wrote that Mrs. Fuller was ill and that she had been requested to visit her. Mrs. Patterson replied that she was not done with her pupilage yet and recommended that Mrs. Fuller visit Dr. Quimby.[2]

All of Dr. Quimby's students had free access to his manuscripts and writings and made numerous copies for their own use. According to Julius A. Dresser, a student of Dr. Quimby, he used to talk hours and hours, week in and week out, the students listening and he patiently answering questions.

Dr. Quimby did not use medicine or any material agency, but worked on scientific principles, the philosophy of which was understood by his students. (Luke 16:17)

2. Letter in Library of Congress.

PHINEAS PARKHURST QUIMBY

Accepting the fact that man rises superior to circumstances, free from the fear of disease, he lives a more natural and happy life.

He taught that the senses, including sight, hearing, sensation, smelling, tasting, are all spiritual—and in reality are attached to Spirit or God, rather than existing in the so-called material structure or natural man which he said was the imitation or shadow of the inner, real scientific man. (II Cor. 5:8) (Deut. 34:7) (Rom. 10:17)

Through this Truth man is enabled to control the body, and make it subservient to the spiritual man whose birthright is dominion, instead of being a slave completely at the mercy of the outer form which he will be if he allows it is subject to disease. (Ps. 8:6)

As we have more of this true knowledge ourselves, we shall love and worship God, who is the source of all wisdom, more sincerely and intelligently. (Prov. 8:11) (Prov. 9:6)

Dr. Quimby states that the visible form is the shadow, but the everlasting substance is not seen in it. He found disease to be an invention of man dominated by error and opinions believed to be true. He lifted disease from its pretended basis of truth and placed it on its proper basis of error. He did not admit disease only as a deception. (Zephaniah 3:15)

The carnal concept with its false beliefs is always a deceiver. (John 8:44)

HIS LIFE AND WHAT HE TAUGHT

Dr. Quimby used to say that he had the same class to uphold him that Jesus had . . . the sick. "The well opposed Him and they oppose me."

Dr. Quimby said, "I do not set myself up as an equal with Jesus or any other, but I do profess to believe in the Principle that Jesus taught which I call Christ. That I do try to put into practice as far as I understand it, and the sick are my judges, not the well. For as the well need no physician they cannot judge me. Neither am I willing to be judged by the creeds till they can show me that their belief is above the natural man."

What does Jesus Himself say of this Power? He admitted it. He says, "Of myself I can do nothing," thus admitting a power superior to Himself. (Ps. 62:11) (I Chron. 29:11) Also, when asked a question of His disciples, He said, "No man knoweth, not the angels in heaven, nor the Son, but my Father only." Ignorance of Christ or Science put Jesus and Christ together and said "Jesus Christ." Jesus was one character, the carpenter of Nazareth, and Christ another. (John 5:30) (John 8:28) The Christians of that day considered Jesus Christ like George Washington, that is a single person with a double name. No one believes that Saul was the surname for it was a Christian name and Paul was the other, yet they did not belong to the same character and we have Paul's own words to prove this testament correct. We also have Jesus' own words to prove that

He was not God, but that the Christ (the spiritual man) was. (John 8:28) (John 5:17)

The people have no idea of God, though it is true they have a belief about God, but it is as absurd as their belief about heaven. They cannot locate Him either in heaven or on earth, or under the earth, and yet they believe in Him.

The great fault is that man has been taught to believe that matter is intelligent and that matter can be developed as can Science or Spirit. This is an error. (John 15:5) (John 9:33)

When Wisdom is acknowledged to contain every idea, and it is acknowledged that nothing can exist without its knowledge, then, although man as we call him, cannot admit it, because of his unbelief, it will not prove that it does not exist. (I Cor. 3:18)

Jesus wanted to introduce the Science He called Christ, which gave the lie to the old opinion of His day. He had no heaven or hell outside of man's consciousness, no happiness or misery except WITHIN. His God was in Him, the kingdom *within,* and within each one of us is the Christ, giving man as the child of God, DOMINION. If this law could be *understood,* it would rid us of all evil beliefs that are bound in the natural or carnal man. (Ps. 19:7) (Prov. 29:18)

Those who seek Him in prayer, desiring to learn His laws will be rewarded in proportion to their labor. (Rom. 10:4) (I Cor. 15:58)

Again Dr. Quimby says, "This is my theory, to put man in possession of a Science that will destroy the false beliefs of the sick, and teach man one living profession of his own True identity with Life, free from error and disease. Therefore, to be free from death is to be alive in Truth, for sin or error is death and Science or Wisdom is eternal Life and this is the Christ." (John 8:36) (Habakkuk 1:13)

Dr. Quimby dissipated from the mind the belief of disease and induced in its place the idea of God which is health. (Ps. 43:5)

In six years he produced ten volumes of manuscript. Subjects all from the standpoint of his theory. Among these subjects were, "Relation of God to Man, Music, Marriage, Science, Wisdom, The Other World, Curing the Sick, Error, Truth, Happiness, Science of Man," and dozens of others. All of his students had free and continuous use of them.

In March, 1860, one of his numerous manuscripts was entitled, "Prayer" and the following is an excerpt taken from this: "True prayer is the desire of the heart, and if the heart is right the prayer will be answered." (Ps. 91:15) (Isa. 65:24)

To worship God is to worship Him in Spirit and in Truth, for He is the Truth. (I John 5:6)

He who expects God to leave Science or Truth and come down to ignorance or error and change Principle for a selfish motive is a knave and knows not God. (Hab. 1:13) (Gal. 3:3)

God is like the fire that throws heat and love, but if we choose to stand out in the cold, we cannot expect exclusive privileges, for God has no respect to one over another. (Acts 10:34) If I act wrongly He does not step out and correct me, I must do it myself. (Col. 3:25)

Jesus had no sympathy with the hypocrite's prayer. He warned His disciples and the multitude against such praying. We are a part of each other and to love our neighbor as ourselves is more than all burnt offering and sacrifices. If you understand this Jesus said you are not far from the kingdom of heaven.

A desire to know God is a desire to know ourselves and that requires our thoughts to come into that happy state of mind that will lead man in the way of health. This is Science and Christ's prayer.

Dr. Quimby taught that if we would conquer and uplift the flesh we must begin by learning how we have helped to make ourselves what we are. We must enter into life in a hopeful spirit, expectant of good, the sound and the sane.

It is within our power so to understand how we have created our ills by false beliefs as to be able to become masters where we were once slaves. Each one of us alone is responsible for what we entertain in our thinking. We may not be altogether responsible for the birds flying over our heads but at least we can prevent their making a nest. What we think is what we are, and all experience is mental, so false beliefs such as fear, sickness, anger, resentment, all carnal beliefs of sin and suffering that man has "invented" must be rooted out. This is the only way to follow St. Paul's admonitions, "to have that Mind that was in Christ Jesus," "To put off the old man with his deeds" and to "put on the new man which is renewed in knowledge after the image of Him that created him." To be "renewed in the spirit of the mind" is to earnestly strive to "have the mind of Christ" which contains and includes every right idea. When we STEADFASTLY "not look on things after the outward appearance then we begin to be in Christ, a new creature, old things are passed away: behold, all things are new." (II Cor. 5:17) (Jer. 10:14)

Dr. Quimby did not believe in a far-off heaven, nor that the "Kingdom of God cometh by observation." (Looking about) (Luke 17:20)

In the words of St. Luke, he believed, "neither shall they say, Lo here; or, lo there; for behold, the kingdom of God is WITHIN YOU." (Luke 17:21) And with St. Paul, "behold NOW is the accepted time. NOW is the day of salvation," and in I John chapter 3, "Behold what manner of love the Father hath bestowed on us that we should be called the sons of God."

To "continue in the Son" is "To pass from death unto life." (John 5:24) THIS is life eternal, "and this is the promise that He hath promised us, even eternal life." (Rom. 8:6)

PHINEAS PARKHURST QUIMBY

Dr. Quimby said, Assure a man that he is a child of God and his soul becomes erect. Man is not in body. (Ps. 56:4) (John 6:63) Jesus gave constant evidence of supremacy of the Spirit over the flesh." (John 17:2)

Jesus or the Christ could put off the body or take it on. (Luke 24:31) He transported cargo and passengers to opposite shore without interval of the boat. He passed through closed doors, multiplied the loaves and fishes, turned the water into wine, brought forth the tax money from the fishes' mouth, proving that what we call matter to be a condensation of Spirit wholly subservient to Mind which is the Christ, according to Dr. Quimby's teaching. (Ps. 8:6) (Gen. 1:26)

The whole of Jesus' teaching was, "BELIEVE," and "as ye believe it shall be done unto you." Dr. Quimby maintained that we are healed through understanding. Explanation, he said, "is the cure." (Prov. 4:5, 6)

Dr. Quimby stated that when Wisdom or Christ spoke through Jesus saying, "Though you destroy this temple, I will build it up again," this that spoke was the Wisdom, so the Builder was not destroyed, but the temple. (the outer form) But the people of that day believed as do many of our day, that the temple and the Builder were the same; so that when the former was destroyed they had no idea of what Christ intended to do. The Christ that acted through

Jesus admitted flesh and blood but His Wisdom knew it was only an idea that He could speak into existence and out. So when they destroyed the idea Jesus, they destroyed to themselves Jesus Christ or Mind in matter. Now when the Wisdom or Christ made Himself manifest to them, they thought He was a Spirit for they believed in spirits but Christ to Himself was the same Jesus as before; for Jesus only means the idea of flesh and blood and all that we call man. Now Christ retained all this and to Himself He had flesh and blood. This was to show that when you think a person dead, he is dead to you BUT *TO HIMSELF* THERE IS NO CHANGE.

When our senses are attached to Truth then we are heirs of Christ and when attached to a belief of mind in so called matter, we are heirs of this world. The Christ is to separate the error from Truth, the tares from the wheat; for Truth is harmony and error discord. (Heb. 3:14)

When God made all things He pronounced them good. (Gen. 1:31) The natural man makes lies and believes them and "as a man thinketh so is he." (Prov. 23:7)

If health and uprightness are the true state of man, and if man has no need to either be sick or unhappy, why is there so much sickness everywhere? The answer is expressed in one word, "OPINION."

Opinion is not Truth, as opinions differ; Truth is always Truth. Opinion is the basis of religious differences and doctors or medical treatments—Truth is one upon which all would agree IF UNDERSTOOD.

The status of mankind is this:—Being born in ignorance and required to work out their own salvation, people have made the natural mistake of judging everything from APPEARANCE. These false beliefs and opinions now form largely the doctrines and knowledge of the world in all departments especially in theology and medicine. (Gal. 4:9)

These systems of formulated opinions and beliefs are constantly changing, showing that they are not the truth of the subjects they refer to.

Henry Ward Beecher, for instance, with reference to the healing of the sick by Jesus and His disciples said that such things were needed then as proofs to a less enlightened age, but are not needed now, yet there are more sick people now and a larger number of diseases.

And Jesus said that ANY man, without reference to time or age of the world who would understand his doctrines should do His works.

We have learned not to judge after the flesh but to prove things by the understanding and the Spirit. (I Thess. 5:21) In as much as we understand, it makes us true sons of God, which is the inheritance into which all men are born. St. Paul said, "With freedom did Christ set us free. Stand fast therefore and be not entangled again in a yoke of bondage." (Gal. 5:1)

Dr. Quimby said that mental attitude is an active cause in determining our condition or the situation we find ourselves in, and either keeps us in it or takes us out of it. We create for ourselves, first mentally then physically what we expect or actually BELIEVE.

Happiness and misery depend upon ourselves.

Many of our diseases spring from excess of one form or another. If thought has been a power for ill, it can now be a power for good. (Zech. 2:13) (Col. 2:10)

Begin now to strive for the Kingdom of God, the consciousness of perfect ideas. WITHIN is the only place we find it. Think on love, harmony, joy, peace, protection, security, and eternal Life and having chosen, STAND FAST, and in due course we will be able to master that which at first seemed impossible. (Gal. 6:9) (Job 22:28)

Self-knowledge, self-control, moderation, poise, and equanimity are not established by affirmation but through realization and understanding. (Prov. 4:7)

Dr. Quimby always said that EXPLANATION was the cure. "To those who build their own world from WITHIN," Dr. Quimby would have said, "it is not your opinion about the world that is of consequence but the ACTUAL Truth of your existence in the world which Wisdom has created. Man has no life or power of his own, no good quality apart from

God, for God alone is the source of Life." (Matt. 19:17) (John 10:10)

Dr. Quimby used the words Science, Truth, Wisdom, Intelligence, and capitalized these words as they were used synonymous with Christ or God. To him the "Science of Christ" was greater than any religion of creeds.

Dr. Quimby maintained that matter is inanimate, there is no Intelligence in it, but it is plastic to thought, and that man should know himself as the scientific or spiritual man, able through Wisdom's help to banish all errors from the world. Life is the knowledge of our existence which has no matter. (John 6:63) (John 15:5) (Jer. 10:23)

God's Mind which was Mind to Christ Jesus is the ONE and ONLY MIND and we are the extension of the Divine Mind, inseparable from this Parent Mind. (John 20:17) (John 10:34, 35) By KNOWING this we get rid of the belief of the carnal mind which the natural man believes to be in the brain. (Phil. 2:5) (Col. 2:18) (Rom. 8:8, 9)

"Cursed be the man that trusteth in man and maketh flesh his arm, whose heart departeth from the Lord." (Jer. 17:5) (Mal. 2:10) When we do this, we incur all the trials and vicissitudes intrinsic to the existence miscalled material. "Cease ye from man whose breath is in his nostrils." (Isa. 2:22) We must begin right where we are thinking to correct that which is "appearing." Divine REALIZATION

HIS LIFE AND WHAT HE TAUGHT

is the goal. We must go back to the basic spiritual pattern or substance which is always mental. We should never attempt to improve the shadows as such but strive to perceive the Truth about the subject. This Truth is always patterned after the Divine. "Thou are of purer eyes than to behold evil, and can'st not look on iniquity." (Hab. 1:13) (Ps. 37:37) (Eccl. 7:29) (I Tim. 4:4)

Every experience is the product of mental formation and all perceptible things are composed of the same elementary substance. This was what Dr. Quimby believed and taught.

Jesus came to give us Life more ABUNDANTLY and as sons of God, His heirs, and joint heirs of Christ, we have a legitimate right to claim our inheritance. To him that "hath" shall be "given." When we perceive the Spiritual Truth or right idea of a condition or situation, we have accepted what is already ours in Spirit, and the externalization corresponds to, or is commensurate with the quality of the mental prototype. We are either victims of fears, opinions, and false beliefs or we may attain our rightful estate by claiming everything that belongs to us. (Gal. 4:7, 30, 31) (Ps. 16:6)

His theory teaches one to recognize what actually exists here and now since God is not somewhere afar off but immanent in His *World of Manifestation* (effect) and in the *soul*. (Jer. 23:23, 24) (Luke 17:21)

PHINEAS PARKHURST QUIMBY

Although Dr. Quimby applied his theory especially to the healing of the sick and the instruction of those who cared to learn about his ideas, it is sufficiently comprehensive to be a guiding factor in every moment of life; it inculcates a mode of life rather than a mere method of healing.

He became more and more convinced that disease was an error of mind and not a real thing, and in this he was misunderstood by some, and accused of attributing the sickness to the imagination, which was the very reverse of the fact.

According to Julius A. Dresser, Dr. Quimby used to say, "If a man feels a pain, he knows he feels it, and there is no imagination about it, but when you learn WHO and WHAT you are, your real self, the spiritual, SCIENTIFIC man will have taken possession of your body, and your world and will transform them into a new heaven and a new earth." (I John 3:1-3) (Rom. 8:6)

HIS LIFE AND WHAT HE TAUGHT

EXCERPTS FROM
DR. QUIMBY'S MANUSCRIPTS

FROM A MANUSCRIPT entitled "Extracts from P. P. Quimby's Writings—"The Science of Man; or the Principle Which Controls All Phenomena."

The extracts follow:

Preface.

In this Science the names are given thus: God is Wisdom and this Wisdom not an individuality but a Principle, which Principle embraces every idea form of which the idea man is the highest. Hence the image of God or the "Principle."

Jesus was the name of a man and Christ was the Truth. This Truth was God and Principle of the idea Jesus. All One.

The Holy Ghost was Science which the Principle sends forth to reveal Truth. This Truth which was Christ was the off-spring of a Principle which was God, the Father. Apply this Science to the idea Man it stands thus;

Wisdom, Love, and Truth is (sic.) the Principle of the idea man and is health. Error is matter and all the sickness that can be is in it, for all would be harmony and health if controlled by Truth. Matter being but a belief is constantly changing. We cannot place the Truth in matter for Truth never changes; hence as Wisdom, Love or Truth is the only Intelligence, it is a Principle outside of matter, and to give Intelligence to matter is an error which is sickness. This is all that can be to sickness. Truth is health. Error is matter. Truth is God. God is right. Error is wrong. These two opposites making God and the devil as used in Scripture and ultimately in Heaven and hell, which are conditions of happiness and misery. Matter has no Intelligence of its own, and to believe that Intelligence is in matter is the error which produces pain and inharmony of all sorts; to hold ourselves we are a Principle, outside of matter, we would not be influenced by the opinions of man held to the working only of a Principle, Truth in which there be no inharmonies of sickness, pain or sin; that the "last enemy to be destroyed is death" are the words of Christ who was Truth —This Science is the opposite of all sin. (I Cor. 15:25, 54, 57, 58)

If I understand how disease originates in the mind and fully believe it, why cannot I cure myself?

Disease being made by our belief or our parents' belief or by public opinion, there is no formula or argument to be adopted, but everyone must fit in their particular case. Therefore it requires great shrewdness or Wisdom to get the better of the error.

I know of no better counsel than Jesus gave to His Disciples when He sent them forth to cast out devils and heal the sick and thus in practice to preach the Truth. "Be ye wise as serpents and harmless as doves." Never get into a passion, but in patience possess ye your soul, and at length you weary out the discord and produce harmony by your Truth destroying error. Then you get the case. Now if you are not afraid to face the error and argue it down, then you can heal the sick.

The patient's disease is in his belief.

Error is sickness. Truth is health. (Jer. 10:15) (Ps. 91:4)

In this Science the names are given: Thus God is Wisdom. This Wisdom not an individuality but is Principle, embracing every idea form of which the idea, man is the highest,—hence the image of God, or the Principle.

Understanding is God.

All Sciences are a part of God.

Truth is God.

There is no other Truth but God.

God is Wisdom.

HIS LIFE AND WHAT HE TAUGHT

God is Principle.

Wisdom, Love, Truth are the Principle.

Error is matter.

Matter has no Intelligence.

To give Intelligence to matter is an error which is sickness.

Matter has no Intelligence of its own and to believe Intelligence is in matter is the error which produces pain and inharmony of all sorts; to hold ourselves we are a Principle outside of matter, we would not be influenced by the opinions of man, but hold to the workings of a Principle, Truth, in which there are no inharmonies of sickness, pain, or sin.

For matter is an error, there being no substance which is Truth in a thing which changes, and is only that which belief makes it. (Job 8:9)

Christ was the Wisdom that knew Truth dwelt not in opinion, and that matter was but opinion that could be formed into any shape, which the belief gave to it, and that the Life which *moved* it came *not from it*, but was outside of it.

Matter has no more Wisdom or Intelligence in it than iron or brass. It is a material for error to manufacture into any false belief that springs up. It is a shadow, or machine whose owner cannot be seen. You see the machine called man, but the owner is out of sight, and never can be seen by the shadow, but is all that contains what is called man.

Now when the machine gets out of order, I tell him (not the machine) where the trouble is and convince him of the fact and then go to work to repair the damage. I have been twenty years repairing these old machines, and I have never called to my aid spirits, medicines, nor any other agencies I have mentioned. I appeal to the OWNER of the machine or body.

PHINEAS PARKHURST QUIMBY

Little children's minds are like mortar that can be molded into whatever form of health and happiness you may please, if you know how to do it. I should as soon think of stopping the revolution of a steam engine by throwing coal on the fire as stopping the operation of the mind by a box of pills or curing disease by medicine. Disease is what follows a belief. The misery contained in the belief shows itself in the shadow and this is called disease. And all kinds of inventions are produced to cure disease. I believe these increase disease. It is like Salem witchcraft, instead of explaining the phenomenon which created disease by ignorance. Disease is not self-existent nor created by God, but is purely an invention of man.

Seven cases out of ten throughout the whole community of old chronic cases are the effects of false impressions produced by medical men, giving to the people that they have spinal diseases, heart or kidney or liver disease, or forty others that I could name, to say nothing of the nervous disorders.

The invention of disease like the invention of fashion has upset the whole community. Diseases are like new fashions, and people are apt to take on a new disease as they are to fall in with any new fashion. If no names were given to the disease or its symptoms, there would be one tenth of the illness there is at the day.

There is nothing in your own system of itself to disturb you; you must look for your enemies in the strangers, (false beliefs or opinions) whom you have permitted to come to your mind. No disease is independent of the mind. Strength is in the knowledge.

The only way to approach and eradicate disease must be through the mind. To know that there is no disease independent of the mind, then the cloud, like shadows vanish as error always will when overpowered by the light of Truth. (I Cor. 13:12) (II Cor. 3:18) (Eph. 2:19)

HIS LIFE AND WHAT HE TAUGHT

This Truth is capable of extensive practical application in all the exigencies of life and we learn to make constant use of it as we advance in knowledge. It helps us to place a just estimate upon everything, the value of life is enhanced, and as we have more of this true knowledge in ourselves we shall love and worship God, who is the source of all Wisdom, more sincerely and intelligently. (I Pet. 3:10) (Prov. 13:14)

FROM DR. QUIMBY'S QUESTIONS AND ANSWERS

Jesus never said He had a spirit but said, "Spirit hath not flesh and bones as you see me have." There was the rock they split upon. Jesus Wisdom knew that this Wisdom was not in the idea body; their knowledge made Mind in and a part of the body. So each reasoned according to his wisdom. Their wisdom was their opinion about what persons had said a thousand years before without any proof but merely as an opinion. This they called knowledge. (Prov. 23:4) (Job 28:12) (Col. 3:10) (I Tim. 2:4)

So far as Christ was concerned all their opinions had no effect. Christ was the Wisdom that knew matter was only an idea that could be formed into any shape and the Life that moved it, came not from it, but was outside of it. Here was where their wisdom differed. How far their idea of Jesus went I am unable to say. Some said He was stolen, others that He rose. Now I take Christ's own words for Truth when He said touching the dead, that they rise. "God is not a God of the dead but of the living." He knew that they could not understand, but to Himself Christ went through no change. To His disciples He died. So when they saw Him they were afraid because they thought He was a spirit, but Christ had not forgotten His identity, Jesus, or flesh and bones. So He says, "A spirit hath not flesh and bones as you see me have." (Luke 24:37, 39)

If Christ's believers could have been there with their present belief, I have my doubts whether they could have seen or heard any sound. (Luke 24:16) Yet I believe Christ did appear and show Himself as dense as their belief, but their unbelief made the idea so rarefied that it was a spirit.

These are my ideas of the resurrection of Christ. Christ lost nothing by the change. *The dead, as they are called, have no idea of themselves as dead.* (Luke 8:52, 55)

When you speak of the natural man, you speak of matter. When you speak of Spirit, you speak of the Wisdom that will live after the matter is destroyed. (Rom. 8:11)

Its happiness and misery are in itself. So the shadow or imitation is the medium of Truth and error. To error it is matter, but to TRUTH it is *shadow*. (Jer. 10:14) (Heb. 6:18, 19)

HIS LIFE AND WHAT HE TAUGHT

EXTRACTS FROM LETTERS WRITTEN BY DR. QUIMBY TO PATIENTS[1]

January 25, 1861

ETERNAL LIFE IS CHRIST. This teaches us that matter is a mere shadow of a substance which the outer, natural man never saw nor can see. This substance is the essence of Wisdom. Matter is dense darkness. Spirit is Light. If you are wise, your body is light, and if you sink into error you become dense and dark. Therefore let your light shine, so that when the wind comes blowing round in the form of an opinion, you may know it is merely the noise of a demagogue. (Titus 2:15) Believe not and you will live and flourish. If you can understand this, you have the basis of my teaching. (II Cor. 10:7) (II Cor. 4:16) (I Peter 3:4)

Two worlds, one opinion, and one Science or Truth. Opinions are matter or the shadow of Truth. One is limited in its sphere, and the other has no limits. One can be seen by the natural eyes, and the other is an endless progression. One is always changing, and the other is always progressing. (Gal. 6:3) (II Cor. 5:17)

The natural man will never know this Truth for he cannot see Wisdom and live. Wisdom is the destruction of the natural man. So he looks upon it as an enemy, prays to It as though the Wisdom were a man. The natural man is a servant or shadow, all an imitation. Science is of another character. Science rises above all narrow beliefs. (II Cor. 10:5) (Jas. 4:8)

He who is scientific in regard to health and happiness is his own law and is not subject to the laws of the natural man except as he is deceived or ignorant. (Gal. 3:13) No

---

1. Quoted from letters in Library of Congress.

one after he knows a Scientific fact can ignorantly disobey it. (Ps. 19:7) So with Science the punishment is in the act. Sin is its own punishment. With man's law it is different; the penalty may follow the act or come after. To know Science is to know Wisdom, and how can a man work out a mathematical problem intelligently and at the same time say he is not aware of the fact. (Proverbs 29:18) (Romans 8:2)

If we know the true meaning of every word or thought, we should know what will follow. So, a person cannot scientifically act amiss, but being misled by opinions, we believe a lie to be true and suffer. (I Cor. 2:14)

The father or author of disease is a hypocrite, a liar and a deceiver. It comes to a person under the most flattering form, with the kindest words, always very polite, ready to lend its aid in any way where it can get a hold. (Prov. 20:17) (Prov. 14:25)

The Prince of hypocrites or carnal mind sometimes comes in the form of a lady or appears as a doctor.

My arguments are aimed at the opinions or *false beliefs*, not at *persons*.

March 10, 1861

Remember what I told you, not lose control of yourself, but stand on deck and give orders not in a whining way, but bold and earnest. Then your crew will obey orders, you will steer clear of all danger and land safe in the port of health. (II Cor. 10:4) (Proverbs 12:18) (Heb. 4:12)

March 19, 1861

The same Christ whom you think Jesus, is the same Christ who stands at the door of your dwelling, knocking to come in, and sit down with the child of Truth (Science) who has

HIS LIFE AND WHAT HE TAUGHT

been led astray by blind guides into the wilderness of darkness. Now wake from your sleep and see if your wisdom is not of this world. (Prov. 20:13) To be born again is to unlearn your errors and embrace the Truth of Christ. (Rom. 13:12) This is the new birth and it cannot be learned except by desire for Truth, that Wisdom that can say to the winds of error and superstition, "Be still" and they will obey. (Heb. 4:12)

I sent back the five dollars till the cure is performed. Till then it is without an equivalent on my part.

I feel certain of success. All I look for is the cure. (Prov. 3:5) (Ps. 103:3)

Our happiness and misery are what follow our belief. As we measure out to another it will be measured out to us again. (Matt. 7:2)

The Science I try to practice is the Science or Christ which was taught 1800 years ago, and has never had a place in the heart of man since, but is in the world, and the world knows it not. Hoping this may limber the cords of your neck. (John 1:10) (Matt. 28:20) (I John 3:24)

PHINEAS PARKHURST QUIMBY

QUOTATIONS FROM THE QUIMBY MANUSCRIPTS

WE MUST TAKE OUR BIBLE as our guide to eternal Life. (Acts 17:11) (Matt. 22:29) (John 5:39)

The natural man is of the dust. (I Cor. 15:47) (Isa. 2:22)

Body is the shadow or imitation of the real man. (I Chron. 29:15)

When Wisdom (spiritual thinking) moulds the clay, error stands aside. (II Cor. 5:8) (Jer. 18:6)

Man leads a life of MIND. (Jer. 10:14) (Gal. 4:31) (Prov. 23:7) (Phil. 2:5)

Jesus was a carpenter. (Mark 6:3) (I Cor. 12:3) (John 5:30)

Christ is God. (Matt. 16:16) (John 10:30) (John 12:44)

The inner man is Christ. (Rom. 8:9) (Rom. 7:22) (I John 4:4)

Whatever we believe, we create. (I Pet. 3:10) (I Cor. 12:7) (Prov. 23:7)

The destruction of false beliefs is *not the annihilation* of so-called matter but error. (Heb. 11:3) (Eph. 5:23) (I Cor. 15:40, 44)

Death does not rob us of our faculties. (John 7:24) (I Cor. 12:22, 23)

Our senses are spiritual and eternal. (I Cor. 12:27) (II Cor. 5:7)

Man's identity is not in what we see, but in the Wisdom which cannot be seen. (Gal. 5:25) (II Cor. 5:6)

We take opinion for Truth. (Jer. 10:23) (Prov. 22:21) (John 8:32)

HIS LIFE AND WHAT HE TAUGHT

An individual is to himself just what he thinks he is. (Isa. 55:7, 8, 13) (Prov. 4:23)

We all have spiritual supremacy over false beliefs. (Rom. 6:14) (I John 4:6) (Eph. 6:17)

Unless a man find the "kingdom within," (the kingdom of right ideas) he can hardly expect to recognize it without. (Matt. 23:26)

Reverse the word EVIL and we have the word LIVE. (Matt. 22:32) (Luke 20:38)

Man is not in the body. (Rom. 8:12) (Rom. 8:9)

Form exists through God's Wisdom. (Luke 24:39) (Isa. 43:21) (John 1:3) (I John 3:2)

The body has no strength of its own. (Ps. 73:26) (John 6:63) (John 15:5)

Life is the knowledge of our existence which has no matter. (John 1:4) (Eph. 4:23)

We can stand at the helm and not allow false opinions of the natural man to guide our barques. (Job 22:28) (Titus 1:13)

The POWER OF WISDOM can condense Mind into a solid so dense as to become *so-called matter*. (Matt. 19:26) (I John 5:7) (John 1:14)

The people confounded the man Jesus with His Power, now they worship the form or shadow of the substance Christ. (John 5:30, 31) (John 6:63)

God made man of ideas. (Ps. 8:6) (Jer. 1:5)

Man is a compound idea. (Ps. 139:17, 18)

The natural man must become subject to the scientific man. (Rom. 13:1) (Phil. 2:2)

When we identify ourselves as God's image, the new birth will begin. (I Thess. 5:5) (John 3:7) (Gen. 9:6)

All effects in the outer world have their cause in the spiritual world. God is the only Creator. (Rom. 1:20) (Col. 1:16)

PHINEAS PARKHURST QUIMBY

God pronounced His creation good. (Gen. 1:31)

When Jesus appeared after the crucifixion He condensed His spiritual self so that it could be seen by the natural eyes and He did it scientifically. (II Tim. 1:10) (John 21:4, 7)

The natural man is of the earth earthy, the spiritual man is of the Lord from heaven. (I Cor. 15:47)

What we do not want in experience must not be entertained in thought. (Luke 12:2) (Isa. 55:7)

God hath made man upright; but they have sought out many inventions. (Eccl. 7:29) (Rom. 1:22)

God's original pattern was perfect but false beliefs and opinions have deceived man. (Gen. 1:26) (Rom. 14:4) (Gen. 17:1)

False beliefs are of the devil (carnal mind) but "there is no Truth in him. He is a liar and the father of it." (John 8:44)

Body is not to be denied but "redeemed." (Rom. 8:23) (I Cor. 12:25-27)

Thoughts are one thing and belief another. If I really believed anything, the effect would follow whether I was consciously thinking of it or not. (Matt. 21:22)

Man is a compound idea and sends forth its fruit whether true or false. The original fruit was perfect; beware of the grafted fruit. (Luke 6:43-45) (Gal. 5:22) (Gen. 1:27)

The sting of ignorance is death. (I John 3:14)

As man dies to his false beliefs he lives in Wisdom. (Rom. 6:11) (Prov. 12:5)

I am in the hands of a merciful God who will do all things right. (Ps. 25:6)

The indwelling Christ. (I John 4:13)

Man is the complete image of the God he ought to worship. (Ps. 82:6) (Gen. 5:1)

Christ acting through man heals the sick. (Mark 9:23) (John 14:12)

HIS LIFE AND WHAT HE TAUGHT

All inflamatory conditions have their seat in the natural man. (Prov. 23:7) (Prov. 12:18) (Isa. 57:4)

All causation is mental or spiritual. (John 1:3) (Heb. 11:3)

Man is an idea of God. (I Pet. 1:16) The Christ within is man's life. (Matt. 5:48) (John 1:12)

The original fruit of the tree of knowledge was spiritual. (Eph. 3:3, 4) (Isa. 25:7)

Be not deceived by the grafted fruit. (Rom. 7:23) (Rom. 7:11) (I Kings 8:27)

Natural man has no life or power of his own. (Col. 2:17) (Rom. 8:11)

Disease is the invention of the carnal man. (Rom. 8:6, 13)

The scientific man must stand on deck and give orders bold and earnest and the natural or carnal man responds. (Prov. 18:21) (I Thess. 5:6) (Job 22:28)

Every person is responsible for his beliefs and must suffer the penalty for them. (II Tim. 2:22) (II Tim. 2:26)

Sin is its own punishment. (Matt. 7:16-17)

There is nothing real about you but Spirit. (I Cor. 14:37, 38) (Luke 3:38)

Nothing cannot cause something. (Isa. 57:4) (Gen. 3:19)

Matter understood is Mind. (Gal. 6:3) (I John 1:25)

To find the indwelling Christ is to put off the old man for the new man. (Rom. 7:22) (Phil. 2:5) (II Cor. 5:17)

Sight is spiritual. (II Cor. 5:7)

Hearing is spiritual. (Rom. 10:17)

All there is to man is spiritual. *Now* are we the Sons of God. (I John 3:2) (Col. 4:12)

As you believe so it is unto you. (Prov. 23:7)

Every experience is the product of mental formation. (II Tim. 2:16) (Mark 4:25)

Man's senses are his life. Life is God. (Job 22:21)

Man's faculties function independent of matter. (II Cor. 5:17)

A man could exist with all his spiritual faculties even if the body were laid aside. (Matt. 16:25)

The outer man is the imitation or shadow of the inner real man. (II Cor. 4:16) (Isa. 57:4)

The indwelling Christ is the substance. (I John 4:15)

The existence of the senses, sight, hearing, touch, smell, taste do not depend on body for their identity. They are spiritual. (John 6:63)

Stomach has no intelligence by which to act or inform us of anything. (Ps. 56:4) (Ps. 62:11)

There is a mental way of making disease and a spiritual way of unmaking it. (Jas. 1:8) (Eph. 5:9, 10)

Man is a compound idea. (Ps. 5:8)

Disease is the shadow of false beliefs. (Prov. 13:17)

We make our own heaven and hell. (Phil. 2:5)

The Christ Mind is heaven. (I Pet. 1:4)

The carnal mind is hell. (Luke 12:29) (Rom. 8:6, 7)

Matter is mental and moulded by MIND. (Heb. 6:19)

The Wisdom of Science is eternal Life. (I Pet. 1:4)

When we find Life in God, the Christ within and lose the belief of life in ourselves, we lose our life and find it. (Matt. 10:39) (Gal. 2:20) (Phil. 3:3)

The earthy man is identified by body and out of the heart of this man proceedeth all evil thoughts. (Rom. 8:6) (Matt. 15:18-21)

Jesus said "flesh and blood" did not reveal the Christ to Peter. (Matt. 16:17)

Our bodies are like machines to be moved. Real body is of Christ, the embodiment of right ideas. (Matt. 16:17) (John 8:28) (I Cor. 12:12-14)

Mind or God is the steam. (Prov. 3:7) (Ps. 119:25)

HIS LIFE AND WHAT HE TAUGHT

Real identity is not flesh and blood. (I Peter 1:24)

The Truth of Christ gives the lie to old opinions (or false beliefs) based on appearances. (II Cor. 3:14) (II Kings 4:20, 26) (Ps. 19:7)

Heaven and hell are within consciousness. (Matt. 5:18) (Ps. 73:25) (Isa. 65:17) (I Cor. 15:50) (Luke 17:21)

We make our own heaven and hell. (Job 25:26) (Jas. 4:7) (Jas. 1:12) (Matt. 16:16, 18) (2 Sam. 22:33)

Matter is inanimate, there is no intelligence in it. (Col. 2:10) (Isa. 40:8) (2 Sam. 23:2) (Rom. 8:2, 4)

God never bound any one. (Heb. all Chap. 11) (Job 12:18)

All the evils that man is heir to are the inventions of the natural or carnal man. (Rom. 8:17) (Eph. 4:27)

Mind, the scientific man must speak and the natural man keep silent. (Eph. 4:31) (Zec. 2:13) (Eph 5:11)

Matter contains no Life. Christ is Life. (I John 5:11)

Matter contains no Truth. Jesus said, "I am the Truth." (John 14:6)

Matter contains no Intelligence. God is Intelligence. (Isa. 40:22) (Isa. 40:17)

Matter is not true AS matter. It is Spirit misconceived. (II Cor. 3:5)

The brain does not think. Mind is the thinker. (Phil. 2:5)

Brains are not Mind. (II Cor. 3:5) (Ps. 94:11) (I Cor. 2:16)

God is Life. (Matt. 10:20)

God is Sight. (Rom. 11:36) (Ps. 94:9) (John 1:4) (Luke 11:34)

Science or God is all five senses supposed to be in the natural body. (Ps. 94:11)

The natural man walks and talks only in belief. (Jer. 10:23) (Col. 2:18) (Gal. 5:25) (Rom. 8:1)

Of himself man can do nothing. Science or God can do all things. (John 14:10) (John 15:5)

The Christ within is the Power. (II Cor. 3:17) (I Cor. 2:5)

All the religion I acknowledge is God or Wisdom. (Prov. 4:2) (Deut. 32:4)

The Son of God or the Christ was sent by God to govern and control the natural man. (Heb. 3:14)

The Christ is the Wonder Child, and the real identity of each of His adopted sons. (Deut. 32:4) (Isa. 9:6)

The scientific man was called "angel" by the natural man. (Dan. 6:22)

There is a war-fare between the natural and scientific man. (II Cor. 10:4) (Eph. 4:13-14)

If the natural man rules, disease and unhappiness are his fate. (St. Mark 7:15) (Phil. 1:27)

If the spiritual or scientific man rules, life and happiness are the result. (Ps. 67:2) (Prov. 29:18) (Prov. 3:13)

Attach the senses to Principle, instead of person, to Spirit, instead of matter. (Matt. 7:24) (II Cor. 3:6) (II Cor. 3:17) (Job 32:21)

Error is death, Truth is Life. The resurrection of one is the destruction of the other. (Matt. 6:24) (John 8:51)

The natural man makes lies and believes them. (I Cor. 2:14) (Jonah 2:8) (Prov. 12:17, 19)

God made all things and pronounced them good. (Gen. 1:31) (Gen. 1:18)

With the axe of Truth I strike at the root of every tree of error, and hew it down so that there shall not be one error in man showing itself as disease. (Ps. 91:4) (Ps. 86:13) (Zec. 8:12)

Your life is your consciousness. (Eph. 4:23) (Rom. 12:2)

The senses exist entirely independent of the body, and if

HIS LIFE AND WHAT HE TAUGHT

we believe taste in the tongue, hearing in the ear, sight in the eye, feeling in the nerves, we must be affected according to our belief. (Rom. 7:5, 6) (Eph. 4:4) (Col. 2:17)

Christ's kingdom is an everlasting kingdom without beginning or end. (II Peter 1:11)

Claim your birth-right as a child of God and Truth will set you free. (John 8:32) (Phil. 4:19) (Ps. 107:35)

The spiritual senses are all there is to man. (Gen. 1:26) (Jas. 1:17)

Life is in the eternal now. (II Cor. 6:2) (John 6:39)

Refuse to admit destructive thoughts. (Phil. 4:8) (I Pet. 2:25) (Prov. 14:25)

The scientific, spiritual man is the Ego. (II Cor. 5:6, 8) (I Sam. 16:7) (Ex. 3:14) (Ps. 107:17)

If a person is found with false beliefs he is arrested and imprisoned. (James 4:7) (Matt. 5:25) (Job 32:18)

Man is ignorant of the fact that he is a sufferer, from his own false belief, not knowingly, but by his own consent. (Ps. 58:3) (Heb. 5:2)

Not being able to judge Cause and effect, he becomes the victim of his own false beliefs. (Col. 1:16) (Ps. 1:1, 2) (Ps. 107:42) (Matt. 6:33)

Man's belief is his heaven or hell. (Ps. 94:11) (Prov. 12:19) (Mark 16:16) (Rom. 14:20)

All that is seen by the natural man is Mind reduced to a state "called" matter. An error of perception, an imitation of the real. (John 1:3) (Luke 3:6)

Christ or spiritual Power existed before the birth of Jesus. It came into the world but could not be seen, and the world knew it not, and it came to its own, and its own received it not. It was Love, Wisdom, Life, Intelligence so it must have an identity, not of matter, but of something else; something that cannot be destroyed and it must be Spirit, God. (Ps. 17:15) (Col. 3:11)

It is the Power which governs all so-called matter whether in the form of man or beast. (I Chron. 29:11) (Ps. 62:11)

As all die in the "old man," (natural) so all are made alive in the "new man" (scientific or spiritual). (Cor. 15:22) (Eph. 4:23, 24)

The time will come when the word "death" will be obsolete. (II Tim. 1:10) (Rev. 21:4)

The realm of ideas is the real world. (Luke 10:9)

Henceforth know we no man after the flesh. (Rom. 9:8) (Acts 17:29) (II Cor. 13:11) (Luke 3:38)

Thought and existence are identical. (Prov. 23:7)

Thinking on the level of the natural man or body is death. (I Peter 1:24, 25) (Gen. 3:19)

The thought of Spirit is Life and peace. (Gal. 5:22, 23) (Ps. 34:13, 14) (Phil. 3:15)

God is the only creator. (Luke 11:40) (Ps. 100:3)

Things are real as Spirit. (Luke 4:18)

The outer man is the natural man. (I Pet. 3:3, 4)

The inner man is the scientific man. (I Sam. 16:7) (Ps. 37:37)

There is only one REAL man, the scientific man. (Jas. 1:25) (Col. 1:28)

I will try to . . . show that (the name) Christ never was intended to be applied to Jesus as a man but to a Truth superior to the natural man. (Matt. 16:17)

The Christ is the God in us all. (I Cor. 3:21, 23) (Col. 1:27)

Where there is no fear there is no torment. Fear is error,

Wisdom casts out fear, for it knows no fear. (Col. 3:15, 16) (Prov. 29:25)

How do we get rid of the natural or carnal man? By finding that the spiritual, scientific man is the ONLY MAN. (Eph. 5:8, 14) (I John 3:24) (Ps. 5:48) (Gal. 6:3) (John 6:39) (II Cor. 5:16, 17)

Signed

P. P. Quimby

PHINEAS PARKHURST QUIMBY

CONCLUSION

DR. QUIMBY LEAVES NO DOUBTS with the reader that false belief or opinion is a decision based on the outer effect or appearance. Understanding is a demonstrable knowledge obtained from a clear concept of the real and eternal. It is existence based on spirituality instead of materiality.

The understanding of man as spiritual, as the embodiment of all right ideas, (God's compound idea) is capable of extricating us from any predicament. Jesus insisted upon a change of consciousness, the renewing of the mind as the only way of salvation from sin, disease and death, and Dr. Quimby has shown us EXACTLY how to do this. (Col. 3:10) i.e. By learning WHO and WHAT we are, through redemption of the natural man, by getting rid of false beliefs, and replacing them with the original spiritual prototype. (Rom. 8:7) (Matt. 12:28) (Eph. 4:23) (Jas. 1:25)

Dr. Raymond Charles Barker, pastor of the First Church of Religious Science in New York City, says in his book, "The Radiant Mentality," that the most important teaching of the New Age is this: "It is absolute Law, that the point of mental attention determines the balance of power." This statement is worth memorizing. (I Tim. 4:15) (Isa. 26:3) (Mark 4:22) (Matt. 12:35) (Job 15:35) (Isa. 65:17)

Dr. Ernest Holmes on 283 of "The Science of Mind," says, "Pray right and God cannot help responding." (Isa. 65:24) (Ps. 99:6) (Luke 11:11, 13) (John 16:24)

The answer must be in the prayer. Cause and effect are spiritually synonymous, and the form that the effect manifests is decided entirely by the form of our acceptance. (St. Mark 11:24) (James 1:6)

In the reality of being exists all we want or need, or can possibly have or wish for. It includes more than we can

HIS LIFE AND WHAT HE TAUGHT

discern in the measure of happiness and the completion of every prayer. This is the spiritual fact and when we consciously ACCEPT what already *belongs* to us in Spirit, we shall receive the tangible proof, for our acceptance decides the appearance. (John 14:14) (Matt. 13:12)

The fact of seeking is the assurance of finding. (Matt. 7:7, 8)

Jesus never disdained the outer manifestations, the loaves and the fishes, but He did admonish His followers to seek FIRST the inner kingdom, the kingdom of Cause, and the effects or signs would naturally follow. We have the divine right to expect this. The two are really one and cannot be separated. (Matt. 6:33) (Matt. 8:13)

Dr. Quimby says that *"True prayer is the desire of the heart."* If we maintain our desires in keeping with the will of God, which is good always, then we will realize health, joy, life and all good. So we watch our desires, thoughts, words, also our beliefs, *rather than body*. (I Cor. 16:13) We are free choosing agents, and can choose Heaven or hell, Life or death, bondage or freedom. (Ps. 16:10) (Isa. 65:17) (Amos 5:14)

To understand how Dr. Quimby healed is to see yourself and others outside the natural man. The scientific man which is the only man there is, is unseen. And when we identify ourselves as God's image and likeness, the new birth begins and we shall begin in very truth to live, speak and think from Him. (Phil. 2:5) (Col. 3:10) (John 3:3)

Fear is the most generally accepted "invention" of the carnal man, and Jesus came on earth to cast out this evil, as well as to liberate the poor and sick. (Ps. 119:45) (II Tim. 1:7) (John 10:10)

Dr. Quimby taught that God's Life is attached to all that we call life, and when the life is detached, the shadow to us is dead, but to God it never had Life. Matter has no more

Wisdom in it than iron or brass. (Prov. 26:12) (I Cor. 3:18) (Dan. 2:20) Man's existence is spiritual and there is no cessation to its spiritual continuity regardless of what the outer pictures say. What we see is nothing but a shadow of Intelligence which is behind the veil or shadow as a man looking in a glass sees himself, but the substance or the real is not seen by the reflection. (Isa. 25:7)

Basing our thought patterns on materiality or appearances produces evil and when based on spiritual facts they create good. "To be spiritually minded is life and peace." (Job 22:21) (Isa. 26:3)

By finding that the scientific (or spiritual) man is the *only* man, we get rid of the false belief of duality. (Rom. 8:9) (Ps. 37:37) In getting rid of the BELIEF of life in shadow, or the imitation called man we lose a false sense of life and find our REAL LIFE in Christ or Spirit. (Ps. 119:104) (John 12:25)

When the false belief is destroyed it leaves nothing else to be rejected and we in truth become the adopted Sons of God. (II Cor. 6:18) (Rom. 8:15) (Gal. 4:5)

Exchanging the false concept for the true does not do away with or deny the body but redeems the body by destroying the misconception or "invention" of the carnal, natural man and reveals the true spiritual identity of body. (Rom. 8:23, 24) "Ye know not what manner of spirit ye are of." (Luke 9:55) (Ps. 8:6) (I John 5:4)

When wrong beliefs are discarded and overcome, all that remains is the spiritual, scientific man and we are that man *NOW*. (Luke 3:6) (II Cor. 6:2)

Each of us must awaken to the Christ consciousness, and cease thinking of himself as a worm of the dust or a material power apart from God. "Ye are the Sons of the living God." (Hosea 1:10) (Ps. 17:15)

Dr. Quimby maintained that health was man's natural

HIS LIFE AND WHAT HE TAUGHT

state, and that only man's false beliefs suggesting impotence and misfortune to his whole self from earliest childhood were responsible for holding the race in the thrall of disease. (Eccl. 7:29) He maintained that a beneficent God could not and would not have created disease and suffering. Only man himself was to blame because of the falsity of his concepts. (Job 13:12)

The process of thinking is the one underlying cause in the life of man, and we became master of our life when we understand that man is spiritual, and bring our thought process under scientific control. (Rev. 2:7)

Dr. Quimby taught his students to rise above pain on Spirits' *wings*. How can one know how to separate the false beliefs from the true? The Truth cannot be changed, the false is always changing. One is Science, the other error, and we can make our choice to attach our senses to Truth which is heaven, or to error or materiality which is hell. (Matt. 45:46)

Man must be taught that he is the author of his own misery, and until that time comes man will be tormented by his own beliefs. We make our own heaven or hell, through spiritual thinking or carnal thoughts. You must face error, see it as an imposter and argue it down with Truth. (Ps. 106:39) (John 8:32) (Jas. 3:6) (Phil. 3:20)

To be set free by Spiritual Truth is to see that Life springs from a single source . . . Christ or Spirit. (John 14:6) (II Cor. 3:5)

Everyone has the possibility of thus entering into Oneness with God. (John 17:11) (Rom. 5:11) (John 10:30) (Luke 10:16)

If you are sick you have the opportunity to use your word, your faith, your courage, and PERSEVERANCE to speak yourself well. (Prov. 18:21) (Mark 16:17)

PHINEAS PARKHURST QUIMBY

So-called matter *understood* is MIND and can be moulded by beliefs, and what we do not want in experience must not be entertained in thought. (Job 10:9) (Luke 3:38)

Nothing can keep us from ruling all error out of thought and so out of experience. We bind ourselves by wrong beliefs alone. (II Cor. 10:5) (II Cor. 3:14)

Dr. Quimby believed that to explain, to understand is to that extent to be free. (Gal. 5:1) (Prov. 4:7)

His contention was not that dead men live again, but that a living man never dies. Life is eternal and this life we are NOW living. "THIS is life eternal." (John 3:15) (Ezek. 19:32) (Isa. 25:8) (II Tim. 1:10)

This was Jesus' religion that Dr. Quimby believed, taught, and practiced to the letter. (Luke 4:18) (Gal. 5:24)

An hour before Dr. Quimby breathed his last, he said to Mr. Dresser, "I am more than ever convinced of the truth of my theory. I am perfectly willing for the change myself, but I know you will feel badly. I do not dread the change anymore than if I were going on a trip to Philadelphia." (Mark 12:27) (I Cor. 15:51) (John 3:15) (John 10:28) (I John 5:11)

This occurred January 16, 1866 at Belfast, Maine. His pupil, Annetta Gertrude Dresser said, "Greater love hath no man than this, that a man lay down his life for his friends. For if ever a man did lay down his life for others, that man was PHINEAS PARKHURST QUIMBY." (II Cor. 6:9) (Rev. 20:6) (Deut. 32:40) (Rom. 6:22) (Rom. 6:9) (II Cor. 9:15)